WORLD ALMANAC® LIBRARY OF
★ THE CIVIL WAR ★

The Civil War in the West (1861–July 1863)

Dale Anderson

WORLD ALMANAC® LIBRARY

Please visit our web site at: www.worldalmanaclibrary.com
For a free color catalog describing World Almanac® Library's
list of high-quality books and multimedia programs,
call 1-800-848-2928 (USA) or 1-800-387-3178 (Canada).
World Almanac® Library's fax: (414) 332-3567.

Library of Congress Cataloging-in-Publication Data

Anderson, Dale, 1953-
     The Civil War in the West (1861-July 1863) / by Dale Anderson.
       p. cm. — (World Almanac Library of the Civil War)
     Includes bibliographical references and index.
     ISBN 0-8368-5583-3 (lib. bdg.)
     ISBN 0-8368-5592-2 (softcover)
     1. West (U.S.)—History—Civil War, 1861-1865—Juvenile
literature. [1. West (U.S.)—History—Civil War, 1861-1865.
2. United States—History—Civil War, 1861-1865.] I. Title.
II. Series.
     E470.9.A53   2004
     973.7'3—dc22   2003062488

First published in 2004 by
World Almanac® Library
330 West Olive Street, Suite 100
Milwaukee, WI 53212 USA

Produced by Discovery Books
Project editor: Geoff Barker
Editors: Betsy Rasmussen and Valerie J. Weber
Designer and page production: Laurie Shock, Shock Design, Inc.
Photo researcher: Rachel Tisdale
Consultant: Andrew Frank, Assistant Professor of History, Florida
     Atlantic University
Maps: Stefan Chabluk
World Almanac® editorial direction: Mark Sachner
World Almanac® art direction: Tammy Gruenewald

Photo credits: Peter Newark's American Pictures: cover, pp. 8, 9, 12, 13,
17, 18, 20, 21, 25, 30, 35, 39 (left), 41 (bottom); Library of Congress:
title page, pp. 2, 14, 22, 27, 32 (bottom), 34, 38, 39 (right), 41 (top);
Corbis: pp. 6, 7, 11, 16, 19, 23, 28 (left), 29, 31, 32 (top), 43.

Printed in the United States of America

1 2 3 4 5 6 7 8 9 08 07 06 05 04

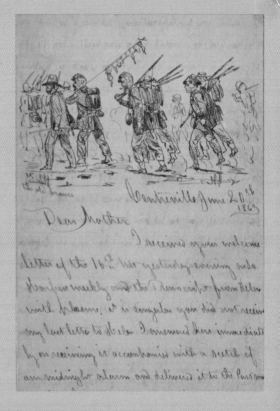

*"To my mother, who got me
Bruce Catton; my brother,
who shared my passion for the
Civil War; and my wife and
sons, who cheerfully put up
with several field trips and
countless anecdotes."*

— Dale Anderson

**Cover: Union soldiers attack Confederate forces at Fort
Donelson. The Union capture of this fort in February 1862
helped secure control of Tennessee.**

Contents

Capital cities
Union States
Confederate States
Seceded from Virginia
Border States
United States Territories

Confederate and Union States in 1861

While the Confederate states covered about as much territory as the Union states, they held fewer people, fewer factories, and fewer railroad tracks and locomotives. These would be significant drawbacks for the Confederacy during the Civil War. The South would also lose part of its support when West Virginia separated from the rest of Virginia in 1863.

The War between the States

The Civil War was fought between 1861 and 1865. It was the bloodiest conflict in United States history, with more soldiers killed and wounded than in any other war. It was also a pivotal event in U.S. history: It transformed the lives of millions of African-American men, women, and children by freeing them from slavery. It also transformed the nation, changing it from a loose confederation of states into a powerful country with a strong central government.

On one side were eleven southern states that had split from the United States to form a new country, the Confederate States of America, led by President Jefferson Davis. They took this step after Abraham Lincoln was elected president of the United

— 4 —

States in 1860. Southerners feared Lincoln would end slavery, which was central to their economy and society. The northern states, or the **Union**, declared this split illegal.

A big question was whether the four **Border States** (Delaware, Maryland, Kentucky, and Missouri) would join the **Confederacy**. They had slavery, too, but they also held many people loyal to the Union. To keep control of these states, Lincoln felt early in the war that he could not risk moving against slavery, fearing that to do so would drive the Border States out of the Union. Later, however, he did declare the emancipation, or freedom, of Southern slaves.

In the Border States, and in many others, families divided sharply, with some men fighting for one side and some for the other. The Civil War has been called a war of "brother against brother."

Fighting broke out on April 12, 1861, when gunners for the South began shelling Union soldiers in Fort Sumter in Charleston Harbor, South Carolina. This attack led Lincoln to call for troops to put down what he called an armed rebellion. Thousands of Northerners flocked to the Union army. Thousands of Southerners joined the Confederate army, determined to win independence for their side.

Soldiers in both the Union and Confederate armies suffered the hardships—and occasional boredom—of life in an army camp. They also fought in huge battles with great bravery and heroism. At times, both sides treated their enemies with honor and respect. At other times, they treated them with cruelty and brutality.

The opposing armies fought in two main areas, or theaters. The eastern theater included Pennsylvania, Virginia, and Maryland; the region near the Confederate capital of Richmond, Virginia; and the Union capital of Washington, D.C. The huge western theater stretched from eastern Kentucky and Tennessee down to the Gulf of Mexico and all the way to New Mexico. By the end of the many bloody battles across these lands, the Union won in 1865, and the states reunited into a single country.

In 1861, many people on both sides believed the war would be short and glorious. By the time of the South's defeat in 1865, however, it had proven long and bloody. The soldiers in the field, of course, were the key factors in the success or failure of the two armies. It was they who won and lost battles. Still, the people at home also did important work to further the war efforts of both the North and the South.

CHAPTER ONE

Early Battles

The chief product of Southern plantations was cotton, shown here piled on the wharves of Brownsville, Texas. The South was among the world's leading producers of cotton, but the success of the trade was made possible only through the use of slave labor.

The Western War

Although the Civil War pitted two clearly defined sides against one another, the war as fought in the West differed from that in the East. First, while both sides wanted to control key cities in the West, they could not hope to quickly end the war by capturing an enemy capital city because both Washington, D.C., and Richmond were in the East.

Second, western commanders had to move troops over greater distances than those in the East. Rivers and railroads allowed both sides to move troops and supplies quickly, which made control over these transportation routes vital. As a result, the armies in the West often tried to seize them.

Third, the armies in the West were generally smaller than the two huge armies in the East, so western battles tended to involve fewer soldiers. Also, in the East, two main armies did most of the fighting, but both sides had several different armies in the West. This meant that battles could occur in different places in the West at the same time.

Fourth, the command situation differed in the West—at least for the Confederacy. President Jefferson Davis never found anyone in whom he had as much confidence as he had in General Robert E. Lee in the East. As a result, he

Warehouses line the bank of the Tennessee River at Chattanooga. The Union army used the warehouses to store supplies that could be shipped along the river or over the nearby bridge.

changed commanders several times and took an active role in their decisions. President Abraham Lincoln spent two years trying to find generals he had confidence in. He finally did in 1863—in both the eastern and the western theaters.

The Confederacy's Goals in the West

Early in the war, the Confederacy had two key goals in the West. The first was to persuade the Border States of Kentucky and Missouri to join with the Confederacy. Both these slave states had strong ties to the South. By convincing them to join the Confederacy, the South would gain men and additional sources of food and supplies. Adding Kentucky and Missouri would also force the Union army to fight over more land. Early in the war, however, the South had only about 50,000 soldiers in the area from the Appalachian Mountains to the upper Mississippi River—too few soldiers to defend so much land.

Nearly seventy-five years old when the Civil War broke out, Lieutenant General Winfield Scott was the U.S. Army's top officer. He developed the Anaconda Plan before resigning late in 1861.

*As the war was breaking out, Winfield Scott—a hero of the Mexican War of 1846 to 1848—commanded the army of the United States. Scott believed that the best way to defeat the Confederacy was to **blockade** its ports and seize control of the Mississippi River. He did not want to rely on huge armies made up of volunteer soldiers led by untested generals. Scott thought that cutting off the South's supplies would speed the Union's victory.*

In the early days of the war, however, many Northerners believed that a stunning victory in battle would end the war and thought Scott's plan was cowardly. They dubbed it the "Anaconda Plan," saying he would strangle the South the way an anaconda squeezes life out of its prey.

In the end, Scott's Anaconda Plan was followed, for much of the action in the western theater consisted of securing the Union's hold on the Mississippi River. That success plus the blockade clearly hurt the Confederacy's ability to obtain supplies. The old general had the last laugh on his critics.

The Confederacy's second goal was to keep control of its rivers; its strategy was to defend its forts and key cities on these rivers from Union force attacks.

The North's Goals in the West

The Union's objectives mirrored the Confederacy's. It focused first on keeping Missouri and Kentucky in the Union. Kentucky was deeply divided, and, at first, the state legislature declared that the state would remain neutral. In September of 1861, however, a Confederate army entered the state of Kentucky from Tennessee, breaking the state's neutrality. The state legislature firmly declared its allegiance to the Union. Southern supporters left the state government and voted to join the Confederacy, but they were in the minority. In the end, both the Confederate and Union armies contained men from Kentucky.

The North's second goal was to control the Cumberland, Tennessee, and Mississippi Rivers. Seizing the Mississippi would split Arkansas, Texas, and much of Louisiana—all west of the river—from the rest of the South. If successful, this would prevent these states from sending supplies to other areas.

Confederate troops under Major General Earl Van Dorn charge a Union position in this view of the fighting at Pea Ridge, Arkansas. Brigadier General Samuel Curtis led the Union army. Feeling betrayed, one Confederate soldier complained, "Nobody was whipped at Pea Ridge but Van Dorn!"

Fighting in Missouri

While Border State Missouri had slavery, many of its citizens were also **Unionists**. Early in 1861, these Unionists formed the majority of a convention held to decide whether to **secede.** It voted against leaving the Union. Still, many Missourians supported the South, and two **militias** formed, one favoring each side of the dispute.

By late summer of 1861, a Confederate force had gathered in southern Missouri. Nathaniel Lyons, the Union commander, decided to march against the Confederates before he lost his army; the volunteers' ninety-day tours of duty would soon end. On August 10, 1861, the two forces met in the Battle of Wilson's Creek. Even though he was outnumbered, Lyons attacked.

— 9 —

DEADLY CONFUSION

The traditional image of the Civil War is of Union soldiers wearing blue and Confederate soldiers in gray. Blue did become the regulation uniform for Northern soldiers, while Southern soldiers wore regulation gray or homemade uniforms dyed brown.

*At the beginning of the war, however, these standards had not yet been established. Uniforms were more varied, and that variety produced some tragic confusion at Wilson's Creek in August 1861. An Iowa **regiment** in Lyons's Union force had gray uniforms. At one point in the battle, attacking Union soldiers came across troops wearing gray. Thinking they had met the Iowan soldiers, they did not shoot. The gray-clad soldiers were Confederates, however, and the Southern soldiers opened fire on the Union troops.*

He was killed in the battle, and his Union soldiers retreated.

Eventually, a larger Union army formed. The Confederate army marched to northeastern Arkansas, where the two forces met at Pea Ridge on May 7–8, 1862. In the heavy fighting, both sides lost about thirteen hundred men, but a strong Union charge drove the Confederates from the field.

Soon after, the remnants of the Confederate force continued east across the Mississippi River to join one of the Southern armies. Their withdrawal gave the Union control of Missouri.

The pro-South **guerrillas**, however, remained a problem in the state throughout the war. From time to time, they attacked Unionists, killing people and burning homes. Some of the famous gunfighters of the West after the Civil War—such as Jesse and Frank James and the Younger brothers—got their start fighting in these guerrilla bands.

The Two Forts

Early in 1862, the war for control of the rivers began in earnest. Ulysses S. Grant of the Union army joined Flag Officer Andrew Foote of the navy in an attack on two forts in Tennessee. Foote's gunboats forced the Confederates to surrender at Fort Henry on the Tennessee River on February 6. Ten days later, Grant and Foote captured Fort Donelson on the Cumberland River. Along with losing the two forts, the South lost more than 14,000 men—a severe blow to already thin western defenses.

With the capture of the two forts, a Union army stood between

At Fort Donelson, Grant showed his aggressiveness. On the first day of fighting, the Confederates had tried, but failed, to break out of the fort. That night, Grant explained why he would attack the next day:

"Some of our men are pretty badly demoralized, but the enemy must be more so, for he has attempted to force his way out, but has fallen back: the one who attacks first now will be victorious and the enemy will have to be in a hurry if he gets ahead of me."

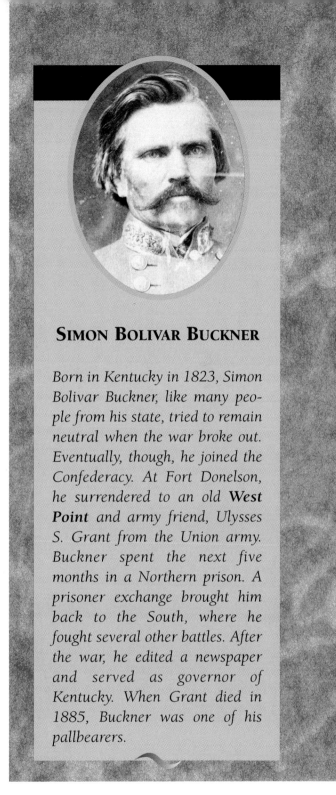

SIMON BOLIVAR BUCKNER

*Born in Kentucky in 1823, Simon Bolivar Buckner, like many people from his state, tried to remain neutral when the war broke out. Eventually, though, he joined the Confederacy. At Fort Donelson, he surrendered to an old **West Point** and army friend, Ulysses S. Grant from the Union army. Buckner spent the next five months in a Northern prison. A prisoner exchange brought him back to the South, where he fought several other battles. After the war, he edited a newspaper and served as governor of Kentucky. When Grant died in 1885, Buckner was one of his pallbearers.*

Confederate forces at Columbus, Kentucky, on the Mississippi River and at Nashville in central Tennessee. An advancing Union army also threatened each of these bases. As a result, the Confederates had to abandon them, giving the Union control of Kentucky and much of Tennessee.

The Union army on the Mississippi River then turned to two other targets. On March 14, 1862, General John Pope won the surrender of a Confederate fort at New Madrid, Missouri. Pope, working with Andrew Foote, then captured the nearby stronghold called Island No. 10 on April 8. Only one fort— Fort Pillow in Tennesse—now stood between the Union army and Memphis, Tennessee.

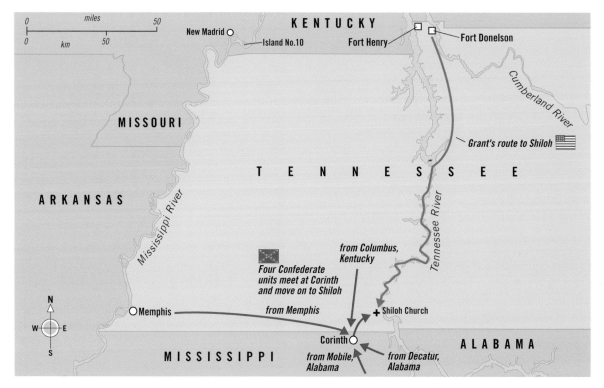

After capturing Fort Henry and Fort Donelson, Grant's army headed south toward Corinth, Mississippi, and camped at Shiloh Church. Albert Johnston combined different Confederate forces to attack Grant there.

The initial Union attack on Fort Donelson was repulsed, but eventually the Confederates had to surrender.

A Wake-Up Call

Gunboats on the Tennessee River (background) shelled the attacking Confederates, helping the Union army hold its positions at Shiloh.

Two Armies Arrive

While Pope was moving down the Mississippi, Union general Grant was marching down the Tennessee River. His goal was to reach Corinth, Mississippi, a vital rail junction where General Albert Sidney Johnston was gathering the Confederate forces. By early April 1862, Grant had reached Pittsburg Landing in southern Tennessee. Nearby stood the Shiloh Church. Marching toward him were 35,000 more Union troops under General Don Carlos Buell. If they joined with Grant's 40,000, the Confederates would be in trouble.

Johnston, meanwhile, had pulled together 45,000 men in Corinth. His second-in-command, General P. G. T. Beauregard, argued that the western

ALBERT SIDNEY JOHNSTON

Albert Sidney Johnston was born in 1803. Before the war, he was widely regarded as one of the U.S. Army's most talented officers. Indeed, he, like Robert E. Lee, was offered command of the entire Union army early in 1861, but also like Lee, Johnston sided with his native South.

A West Point graduate, Johnston had resigned from the army after eight years. In 1836, he joined the Texas rebellion against Mexico. Entering the Texan army as a private, he became a general. He fought in the Mexican War (1846–1848), where he impressed General Zachary Taylor, who brought him back into the U.S. Army. In 1861, Confederate president Jefferson Davis gave Johnston command of the western theater for the Confederacy. After early losses there, many Southerners complained about Johnston. Davis backed him, saying, "If Sidney Johnston is not a general, I have none."

Johnston was wounded in a leg artery at Shiloh in 1862. Having sent his surgeon to care for other wounded soldiers, including Northerners, Johnston quickly bled to death.

armies needed a victory after a string of defeats. "We must do something," he said, "or . . . all will shortly be lost." Johnston agreed, and the two planned an attack on Grant's force before Buell's army arrived. They reached the area around Pittsburg Landing and got all the troops in position on April 5, 1862.

Both Grant's and Johnston's armies were inexperienced, however. Johnston's march had been disorganized and undisciplined, while Grant's forces were completely unprepared for any attack. The Northerners expected Buell's men to arrive any day. Then, they believed, there would be a quick march to Corinth and an easy victory over a demoralized enemy, an enemy whose confidence had weakened.

Surprise Attack

As the Union soldiers ate their breakfast at Shiloh on April 6, 1862, the Confederates broke through the woods in a stunning, powerful attack. Johnston threw all six of his **divisions** into the battle. To meet it, Grant only

had five. In fact, Grant was not even on the battlefield when the attack came; he was at his headquarters a few miles downriver. He quickly took a boat to the scene, however, and took charge of the battle.

The fighting was far fiercer than anything in the war until then, overwhelming some of the inexperienced troops on both sides. Soldiers from both armies broke from the front lines and ran to the rear. Grant and Johnston and their division commanders had to rally their troops, encouraging them to "stand fast," meaning to continue the attack. Many were wounded in the ongoing fire. In the midst of the fighting, General Albert Johnston was shot, and General Beauregard took charge of the Confederate force.

The South's attack at Shiloh was a complete surprise. Confederate general Braxton Bragg described the scene:

"The enemy was found utterly unprepared, many being surprised and captured in their tents, and others, though on the outside, in costumes better fitted to the bedchamber than to the battlefield."

Saving the Day

The heavy attack pushed most of the Union line back 2 miles (3 kilometers). Only Brigadier General Benjamin Prentiss's division held its ground in an area called the Hornet's Nest. The Confederates repeatedly smashed against them,

ULYSSES S. GRANT

Ulysses S. Grant was born in 1822 in Ohio. A quiet, unassuming man, Grant had reached West Point as a replacement for a dropout. On his arrival, he found that his name had been changed, mistakenly, from Hiram Ulysses Grant to Ulysses Simpson Grant. Rather than complain, he accepted the change. Grant did not make a very impressive cadet. However, he graduated, joined the army, and fought with distinction in the Mexican War (1846–1848).

Peacetime army life was difficult on Grant, who began drinking heavily. Rumors of his alcohol abuse forced him to resign. As a civilian, he failed at several different occupations. When the Civil War broke out, he was working as a clerk in his family's store. However, because he was a trained officer, he was commissioned a brigadier general. Throughout the war, Grant remained an aggressive fighter who moved quickly and pounded enemy forces with constant, strong attacks. Hailed as a hero when the Union won the war, he was elected president for two terms. He developed throat cancer after leaving office and died in 1885.

This Union battery—a collection of cannons—was in the thick of the Hornet's Nest fighting.

but the Union soldiers beat back each assault. By late afternoon, Prentiss finally had to surrender. Still, his stand had given Grant time to form a new line. Night fell—and so did a steady rain that added to the two armies' misery.

Having solidified his defenses—and with two divisions of fresh troops—Grant was ready for the next day. An officer suggested that the army retreat. Grant replied, "No. I propose to attack at daylight and whip them." Beauregard was equally optimistic, believing the South had won "a complete victory."

The Second Day

As day broke on April 7, 1862, Grant's army attacked the Confederates all along the line, surprising the Southern soldiers who thought they had won a victory the day before. Slowly, the Union army pushed the Confederates back. By midafternoon, it was clear that the Southern troops were beaten.

LEW WALLACE'S LITERARY CAREER

One of Grant's division commanders at Shiloh was Lew Wallace. Before the Civil War, he had been a reporter, lawyer, soldier, and legislator. After the war, he became governor of New Mexico Territory and ambassador to Turkey. Wallace is best remembered, though, as the author of a famous novel, Ben-Hur. *The novel, set in the Roman Empire at the time of Christ, was a big seller in the late 1800s and has been made into a movie twice.*

General Beauregard called for his troops to retreat before his army could be destroyed.

After the Battle

In terms of **casualties**, Shiloh was the first major battle of the Civil War; the heavy losses horrified people. A total of nearly 24,000 troops were killed or wounded at Shiloh—more than all U.S. casualties in the Revolutionary War, the War of 1812, and the Mexican War of 1846 to 1848 combined.

The soldiers were shocked as well. Grant described the battlefield: "I saw an open field so covered with dead that it would have been possible to walk across the clearing, in any direction, stepping on dead bodies, without a foot touching the ground." A Confederate soldier wrote, "This night of horrors will haunt me to my grave."

General Grant received heavy criticism for being surprised by the Confederate attack. Reports accused him of being unprepared—and even of being drunk. President Lincoln, though, was impressed by how the general had recovered. "I can't spare this man," the president said. "He fights."

War in the Far West and the Southwest

In the Red River campaign—as in other actions in the West—Union armies had to put up temporary bridges to move troops across rivers. Union army engineers became expert bridge builders during the Civil War, usually constructing them faster than the Confederates could destroy them.

To New Mexico and Back

Early in the war, a small Confederate force moved out of western Texas and seized a fort in New Mexico. Its commander proclaimed the southern part of New Mexico and Arizona as a territory of the Confederacy. The Confederates hoped to use this area as a launchpad for further moves to California and Colorado.

THE NATIVE AMERICANS' CIVIL WAR

Some Native Americans fought in the Civil War. Though the exact number is unknown, estimates range as high as 6,000 for the Union and 12,000 for the Confederates.

Many of those recruits were from the "Five Civilized Tribes"—the Cherokees, Chickasaws, Choctaws, Creeks, and Seminoles—who had been forced to leave the Southeast for present-day Oklahoma in the 1830s. Cherokee Stand Watie led a sizeable number of Native Americans in a Confederate unit called the First Cherokee Mounted Rifles. They fought in several battles, from Wilson's Creek in August 1861 until the end of the war. They frequently raided Union supply trains and in one raid grabbed $1.5 million in Union supplies. Watie became a Confederate brigadier general.

Some Native Americans from Virginia and North Carolina helped the Union cause as scouts and river pilots. A Native American unit from Michigan fought in several battles in Virginia. In one, they captured a few hundred enemy soldiers. The most accomplished Native American in a Union uniform was probably Ely Parker, a Seneca. Parker had befriended Ulysses Grant before the war and served Grant as a staff officer until the end of the war.

Many Native Americans stayed out of the war but saw the conflict as a chance to get back their land while the Union army was preoccupied fighting the Confederacy. However, the war did not end Native American suffering. Union Colonel J. M. Chivington led nine hundred white militia against an Indian camp at Sand Creek in Colorado in 1864, killing nearly five hundred Arapahos and Cheyennes, including women and children. An 1863 **campaign** led by Kit Carson broke Navajo resistance in the Southwest. The following year, Carson attacked Comanches and Kiowas in northern Texas but was unable to defeat them.

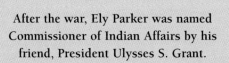

After the war, Ely Parker was named Commissioner of Indian Affairs by his friend, President Ulysses S. Grant.

A bolder stroke soon followed. Confederate brigadier general Henry H. Sibley recruited a force of just less than four thousand men. In early 1862, they set out from Texas to take control of northern Arizona and New Mexico. Sibley's troops defeated a Union force at the Battle of Valverde in northeastern New Mexico, then captured Albuquerque and Santa Fe. Though they were running short of supplies, they won another battle at Glorieta Pass on March 26, 1862. A Union raid burned their remaining supplies, however, and Sibley was forced to return home.

By May, what was left of Sibley's force reached Texas, having lost hundreds of men on the return trip. Confederate dreams of seizing New Mexico were dashed.

Texas in the War

To the Confederacy, Texas could be important as a supplier of food for its armies. Also, its ports could be used to ship cotton, thus gaining money to buy more supplies.

THE ALAMO, SAN ANTONIO, GENERAL TWIGGS'S HEAD-QUARTERS.

Early in 1861, the Confederate flag was raised over San Antonio's famous Alamo, when Texas joined the South.

Thomas North, a Northerner, spent much of the Civil War in Texas. After the war, he described the Union capture of Galveston in 1862 and the Confederate recapture of the city on January 1, 1863. North dismissed the original Confederate commander of Galveston, General Paul Octave Hébert, as "a man of no military force or practical genius." When a small Union fleet attacked, North wrote, Hébert fled like a coward with most of his force rather than defending the city.

Replacing Hébert was Major General John Magruder, who rigged a few old ships as gunboats, covering their sides with cotton bales to protect them from Union shells. Magruder launched a surprise attack at dawn on January 1. One of his makeshift gunboats rammed the most powerful Union ship, and soon after, the Union fleet surrendered.

After the surrender, the commander of the Confederate ram found that his son, the second-in-command of the Union boat, was dying of his wounds. The father cradled his son, who died in his arms. The next day, the father read the burial service for his son. "The victory and defeat were alike forgotten," North added, "under the sublime touch of a human scene so tender."

Paul Octave Hébert was unable to defend Galveston from Union attack.

Union troops captured Brownsville, Texas, in November 1863. The following summer, Southern forces retook the port and reopened trade with Mexico.

Therefore, the Union navy tried to shut down several Texas ports with its blockades. In late 1862, the navy went further and seized Galveston. A few months later, however, in 1863, the Confederate Army won this key port back.

The Union army made another attempt to shut down trade in Texas when it tried a combined land and water action against a Confederate fort along the Sabine River in eastern Texas. Southern gunners at the fort sank two of the four attacking gunboats, though, and the Union force withdrew.

Most of Texas, then, remained in Southern hands throughout the war. Because the North eventually gained control of the Mississippi River, though, this fact did little to help the Confederate war effort. In the end, Texas remained on the margin of the Civil War, and the South could not rely on it for needed supplies.

JOHN WILLIAM DE FOREST

Born in 1826 in Connecticut, John William De Forest became a writer before the Civil War, living part of each year in Charleston, South Carolina, where he observed Southern society firsthand. De Forest and his wife were on the last boat to leave Charleston before the shelling of Fort Sumter began.

De Forest enlisted in the Union army and became a captain. He served for three years, taking part in the Union victory at Port Hudson, the Red River campaign, and fighting in Virginia. After the war, De Forest served in the **Freedmen's Bureau** *in the South for three years.*

He also returned to writing, publishing his major novel, Miss Ravenel's Conversion from Secession to Loyalty, *in 1867. In the novel, Southern-born and Confederate-loyalist Miss Lillie Ravenel marries the Union soldier Edward Colbourne from New England. Their marriage reflects De Forest's wish that North and South could reconcile after the many years of war. De Forest published several other novels, none of which were big sellers. He died in 1906.*

The Red River Campaign

The last major action west of the Mississippi came in early 1864. Union general Nathaniel Banks led a force of nearly 30,000 troops from southern Louisiana up the Mississippi River to the Red River in Louisiana. Then the force moved northwest, hoping to seize Shreveport, Louisiana, and use it as a base to take eastern Texas. Banks was supposed to join with another Union army coming down from Little Rock, Arkansas.

The plan failed miserably; the Confederates won a battle over the Union force in Arkansas, preventing it from joining Banks. Banks almost got to Shreveport but then lost a battle at Mansfield, Louisiana. He quickly began to pull back, but the Confederates attacked several times on this return trip. By mid-May, the campaign was over, and northern Louisiana and eastern Texas remained in Confederate hands.

Union Gains on the Mississippi

~

CHAPTER FOUR

Confederate guns from the two forts guarding New Orleans blaze away
at the Union fleet, which fires back.

The Situation in Early 1862

Control of the Mississippi River was a key goal for both sides in the western theater because it could be used to move troops and supplies. Also, states in the
Old Northwest—such as Illinois and Wisconsin—had long relied on the
Mississippi to ship their farm products to New Orleans and from there to other
countries. Political leaders in those states wanted the Mississippi in Union
hands so the shipments could resume.

By late spring of 1862, the Union army had enjoyed several successes in the West. Though guerrilla warfare continued in Missouri, that important state was in Union control, as was Kentucky. Most of Tennessee was in Union hands, and the Confederate army in the West had been badly mauled at Shiloh. Union forces on the Mississippi River were ready to threaten Memphis, Tennessee. Though the Confederacy still controlled the central Mississippi River and its southern end, the Union navy was ready to challenge that control.

New Orleans: Strategic and Vulnerable

The first strike came against New Orleans. It was a key point—the South's main port and the spot that controlled the entire lower Mississippi River.

It was also vulnerable. Few Confederate ships on the Mississippi River protected the city; most had been sent north to guard Memphis. The Confederates, however, had confidence in the city's main defenses—two forts, named Fort St. Philip and Fort Jackson, about 75 miles (120 km) downriver. The Confederates believed that the forts' guns could sink any ships that tried to pass them. As an added measure,

they chained together the hulls of several old ships, stretching them across the river to block the channel. Union naval commanders had realized from other battles, however, that by massing ships they could overcome the firepower of the forts.

In April 1862, the Union navy attacked. For five days, boats carrying mortars lobbed shells—as many as three thousand each day—into the two forts. The mortars had little effect, however, so the Union commander, Captain David Farragut, decided to run his ships past the forts. One Union boat steamed upriver, and the crew managed—under heavy fire—to break the chain and open enough space in the river for one Union ship to pass at a time.

On April 24, the ships moved forward. The noise, fire, and smoke were intense; hundreds of guns were going off at the same time. Some Confederate ships tried to sink Union ships by ramming them. Other ships were set on fire and aimed at the Union fleet, hoping to turn it into a fiery inferno.

It took an hour and a half of intense action for the Union fleet to pass—but pass it did. Once Farragut's ships reached New Orleans, the city quickly fell into Union hands.

A part of the Fifth Ohio regiment of the Union army entering Memphis on June 6, 1862, is shown here.

More Union Victories

Within a few weeks, the Union navy captured Baton Rouge, Louisiana, and Natchez, Mississippi. Farther upriver, the Confederates were forced to abandon Fort Pillow, Tennessee, in May by the approach of a Northern fleet that was too strong for the fort's guns. A fleet commanded by Charles Ellet captured Memphis, Tennessee, on June 6, 1862. This fleet included nine members of the Ellet family. They quickly defeated the small Confederate vessels sent up from New Orleans, sinking, severely damaging, or capturing all but one ship. A crowd of Southerners watched the defeat of their little fleet with dismay from the river's bank. When Union troops occupied the city, Elizabeth Meriwether of Memphis wrote, "We felt as if chains were encircling us."

Vicksburg Defiant

Union captain Farragut wanted to press his victory on the lower Mississippi by going after the next major Confederate strong point— Vicksburg, Mississippi. Union ships

David Glasgow Farragut had first entered the navy in his early teens during the War of 1812 against Britain.

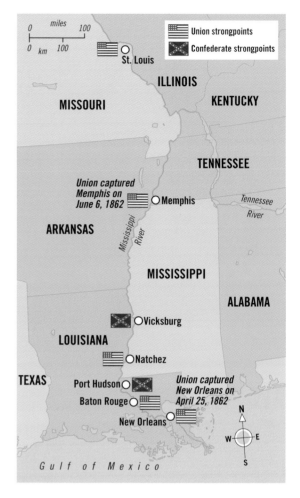

After the Union captured New Orleans and Memphis, the South controlled only the central section of the Mississippi River.

steamed upriver to that city, and their commander demanded that it surrender. On May 18, 1862, Confederate commander general Martin Luther Smith responded defiantly: "Mississippians don't know, and refuse to learn, how to surrender. . . . If Commodore Farragut . . . can teach them, let [him] come and try."

Try Farragut did, but he could not take the city. Its guns—high on a bluff on the eastern bank of the Mississippi—could not be silenced by Farragut's ships. Vicksburg and Port Hudson, farther south, remained in Confederate hands, preventing the North from controlling the entire Mississippi River.

CHAPTER FIVE

Confederate Counterpunch

~

Confederate attacks on Corinth (shown here) and Iuka—and the need to guard railroad supplies—prevented Grant from taking any stronger offensive action.

The Union Army Stalls

While the Union's navy was enjoying success on the Mississippi River, its army was having problems on land. After Shiloh, Major General Henry Halleck arrived in southwest Tennessee. The Union commander for the western theater, he had decided to take personal control of his army. He enlarged the Union force to nearly 110,000 and set off for Beauregard's 66,000 Confederates in Corinth, Mississippi.

Halleck had been spooked, however, by the Confederates' surprise attack at Shiloh. After each day's march, he ordered his men to dig trenches to protect themselves. The advance on Corinth was painstakingly slow—merely 1 mile (2 km) a day.

HENRY HALLECK

Henry Halleck was born in 1815. Nicknamed "Old Brains," he was supposed to have one of the best military minds in the army before the Civil War. Graduating near the top of his West Point class, he wrote a book on the principles of warfare.

Soon after the Civil War began, Halleck was given command of all the Union forces in the West. Though a good administrator, he was not really responsible for the early successes there. Lincoln did not realize this, however, and brought Halleck to Washington as the commander of all Union armies. "Old Brains" remained skilled at organizing and equipping armies but had little feel for strategy. Secretary of the Navy Gideon Welles wrote scathingly that Halleck "originates nothing, anticipates nothing . . . takes no responsibility, plans nothing, suggests nothing, [and] is good for nothing." Halleck remained in the army until his death in 1872.

Eventually, though, Halleck's army reached Corinth. Knowing he could not stop such a large army, Beauregard abandoned the city on the night of May 29, 1862. A few weeks later, he lost command of the army he had saved; Jefferson Davis replaced him with General Braxton Bragg.

Iuka and Corinth

Halleck worried; he thought the army needed to effectively control all the land it had taken so far. He split his army into smaller chunks and sent those pieces in different directions. Don Carlos Buell and his troops were sent to eastern Tennessee toward Chattanooga. Buell moved slowly, though, partly because frequent Confederate cavalry raids harassed his troops, breaking up his supply lines.

Meanwhile, Grant was forced to contend with two small Confederate armies. These armies struck at Union troops at Iuka and Corinth, two railroad junctions in northern Mississippi. The Union forces were able to push the Confederates back.

The South Invades the North

In the fall of 1862, Braxton Bragg boldly launched an invasion of the North at about the same time that Robert E. Lee moved his Confederate army to invade Maryland in the East.

Union armies used steamships to carry supplies along western rivers.

The invasions had similar goals. The South hoped that military success would persuade European countries to recognize Southern independence. Both commanders also hoped to win support—including new recruits—from a Border State. Bragg hoped to gain this support in Kentucky, where many Southern sympathizers lived.

So, setting out from Chattanooga on a westward arc with about 30,000 men, Bragg moved his army north to Kentucky. Another Confederate force—20,000 men under Major General Edmund Kirby Smith—took off on an eastern arc. The two forces were to meet near the Ohio River.

Opposing Bragg were about 55,000 men under Major General Buell. For weeks, Buell had received

When Bragg touched Kentucky soil, he tried to rally support for the Confederacy from the state's people. He issued a high-sounding declaration:

"Kentuckians, I have entered your State . . . to restore to you the liberties of which you have been deprived by a cruel and relentless foe. . . . If you choose . . . to come within the folds of our brotherhood [the Confederacy], then . . . lend your willing hands to secure you in your heritage of liberty."

BRAXTON BRAGG

Born in North Carolina in 1817, Braxton Bragg had graduated near the top of his West Point class. He fought well in the Mexican War, where he received three field promotions. In late 1861, he was made a major general for the Confederacy and sent to the western theater. After Shiloh, he became the commander of the South's main western army.

Bragg had a well-deserved reputation for being prickly and argumentative, frequently bickering with those serving under him. These conflicts hurt his army's performance in battle. President Davis continued to support him, however, and Bragg won promotion to full general, one of only eight Confederates given that rank. In 1864, Bragg came to Richmond to serve as Davis's military adviser. His job had no clear responsibility, though, and he served out the remainder of the war with little to do. He died in 1876.

constant criticism for not moving quickly on his march to Chattanooga. Once Buell realized that Bragg had reached Kentucky, though, he went after the Confederate army quickly.

Southern Gains and Difficulties

Bragg's invasion achieved some early successes. Sweeping aside a small, inexperienced Union force, Smith took Richmond, Kentucky, in late August. A few days later, he seized Lexington, Kentucky. On September 17, 1862, Bragg forced a Union surrender at Mumfordville, Kentucky.

Meanwhile, many people north of the Ohio River became alarmed at the advancing Southern troops.

Don Carlos Buell was blasted by his superiors. One telegram from Halleck said that Lincoln found Buell's slow pace "not satisfactory." Less than a week later, Lincoln's assessment worsened to "great dissatisfaction."

Militias began drilling in Cincinnati, Ohio, and Indiana's governor called for volunteers to defend that state.

Bragg had problems, however. Buell was moving quickly to catch up to him, and his Union troops outnumbered Bragg's force. Further, the fighting men of Kentucky were not flocking to his army. Bragg sent word to Smith that they should join their forces so they could fight Buell.

Southern Defeat at Perryville

Bragg's and Smith's armies united near the town of Perryville, Kentucky. On October 8, Bragg's army, searching for water in nearby Doctor's Creek, ran into Buell's men accidentally, and a battle erupted, marked by great confusion. Bragg did not know at first that he was facing the major part of Buell's army. Buell, in turn, did not realize that part of his force was heavily engaged. Strangely, the wind and the area's terrain prevented him from hearing the sounds of battle. As a result, he did not make full use of all of his army.

When Bragg realized he was outnumbered, he decided to withdraw. Though Buell's army suffered more casualties than Bragg's—about forty-two hundred compared to fewer than thirty-five hundred—Perryville was, in effect, a Union victory. With

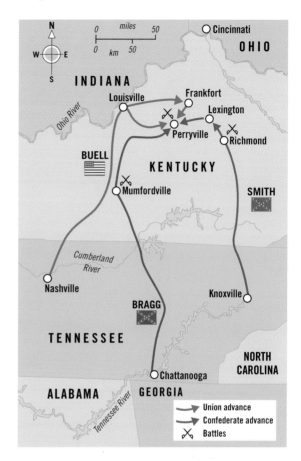

Bragg and Smith set out from Tennessee to launch the Confederate invasion of Kentucky in the fall of 1862. Buell had to pull back from Nashville to meet the threat to areas along the Ohio River.

no Kentucky recruits and faced with a stronger army, Bragg decided he could not stay in the area; his army turned south and marched home.

Bragg was widely criticized for his withdrawal. One of his division commanders told President Davis that Bragg should be removed from command. Still believing in Bragg, Davis refused to do so but did name Joseph Johnston as commander of the entire western theater.

CHAPTER SIX

The Union Moves South

Raiding cavalry often destroyed rail lines, forcing armies to send out crews to repair them.

A New Commander

While General Braxton Bragg's Confederate army moved south, Union general Don Carlos Buell cautiously pursued him. Exasperated by the slow advance, Lincoln believed strongly that the war needed to be pursued vigorously and aggressively. Once more, messages from Washington bombarded the general, urging him to move more quickly. "Neither the Government nor the country can endure these repeated delays," Halleck warned Buell in one telegram.

Buell did not take the hint and did nothing to take the offensive. Finally, on October 24, 1862, Lincoln replaced Buell with Major General William Rosecrans.

On to Murfreesboro

Rosecrans took several weeks to reorganize and outfit his army before, in late December, he finally moved. His army numbered about 42,000. His target—Bragg and his 34,000 men—was about 30 miles (50 km) away in central Tennessee.

Rosecrans and his men were in position just north of the Confederate troops, by December 30, 1862. Bragg's Confederates formed an arc that reached from the north to the west of the nearby town of Murfreesboro, Tennessee.

A cold, steady rain had been falling for several days, and the Union troops were chilled to the bone. Their mood was not improved by being told not to light any campfires, which would have revealed their position to the enemy. The Confederate army, meanwhile, was plagued by ill feeling between Bragg and his division commanders.

Battle Plans

The two commanders developed battle plans that mirrored each other. Rosecrans wanted to use his left to attack Bragg's right, which was the only part of Bragg's line east of Stones River; the rest of his force was west of the water. Rosecrans hoped to crush this force and then turn on the rest of Bragg's army.

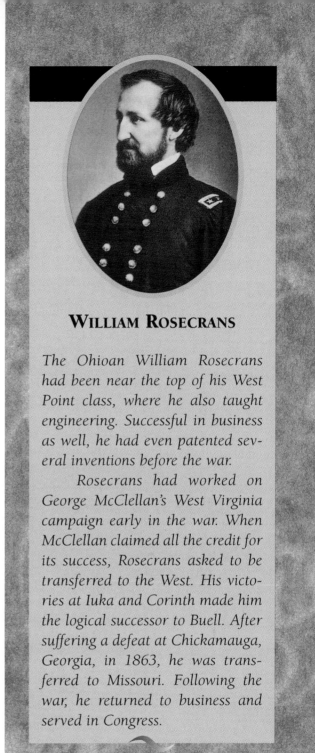

WILLIAM ROSECRANS

The Ohioan William Rosecrans had been near the top of his West Point class, where he also taught engineering. Successful in business as well, he had even patented several inventions before the war.

Rosecrans had worked on George McClellan's West Virginia campaign early in the war. When McClellan claimed all the credit for its success, Rosecrans asked to be transferred to the West. His victories at Iuka and Corinth made him the logical successor to Buell. After suffering a defeat at Chickamauga, Georgia, in 1863, he was transferred to Missouri. Following the war, he returned to business and served in Congress.

Bragg planned to use his left to attack Rosecrans's right. He, too, wanted to sweep around that part of the enemy army and then scatter the rest.

The First Day of Battle

As December 31 dawned, Bragg struck first. His surprise attack stunned the Union soldiers, and the right of Rosecrans's line crumbled. General Philip Sheridan's division stood firm, however, giving Rosecrans time to adapt. He gave up on his idea of attacking and pulled troops from his left to defend his right. He formed a new line perpendicular to the original, shaping it into a hook.

The Confederates kept attacking this new line, but Union cannons pounded them as they came. As darkness fell, the armies stopped fighting. It had been a long and bloody day, and, as Bragg explained, "both armies, exhausted by a conflict of full ten hours' duration, rarely surpassed for its continued intensity and heavy losses sustained, sunk to rest with the sun."

The Second Day of Battle

The two armies rested on January 1, 1863, with only some sporadic firing. In the new positions, the Union army kept just one division east of the river and the rest to the west. Bragg decided to go after that lone division on the Union left. Major General John Breckinridge was ordered to attack it. Breckinridge protested, convinced that Union **artillery** would blast his men as they advanced. Bragg insisted he move, and early on January 2, he did.

His men succeeded in pushing the Union division out of its position, but in their excitement, they overran it, which brought them squarely into the range of the Union cannons blasting away. Breckinridge's division suffered heavy losses, as fifteen hundred were killed or wounded in less than an hour. Bragg called off any further action.

Stones River was a very bloody battle. Both armies lost about one-third of their men, about 13,000 Northern soldiers and 10,300 Southern ones. Bragg had declared a Southern victory after the first day, but it was he who withdrew from the field.

SERENADING

On the night of December 30–31, 1863, while Rosecrans and Bragg prepared their plans, bands with the Union army began playing patriotic tunes such as "Yankee Doodle" and "Hail Columbia." The Southern bands struck back with their own songs, including "Dixie" and "The Bonnie Blue Flag." Eventually, one band started to play "Home Sweet Home." Soon the others joined in, and soldiers in both camps sang. After that sentimental song ended, the armies went to sleep. The next day, they began fighting.

The Mississippi in Union Hands

CHAPTER SEVEN

Grant's difficulties in taking Vicksburg led
to intense criticism. In 1863, General Cadwallader
Washburn complained to his brother, a member of Congress:

*"Grant has no plans for taking Vicksburg.
He is frittering away time and strength to
no purpose. The truth must be told even if
it hurts. You cannot make a silk
purse out of a sow's ear."*

Vicksburg—the Key

Vicksburg, Mississippi, was important to both North and South. As long as the Confederates held the city, the Union navy could not use the Mississippi River at will. While some ships dared to run past the city's powerful guns, regular shipment of troops or supplies up and down the river was impossible with the city in Confederate hands.

The Confederacy could also use Vicksburg to funnel supplies from Arkansas and Texas to areas east of the Mississippi River. Vicksburg was a railroad center as well as a river port. The South could receive goods at the port and move them by train to its armies in the field.

The Geography of Vicksburg

While the Union army wanted to capture Vicksburg, the land in and around the city favored its defenders. Vicksburg sat high on bluffs on the river's east bank, and its powerful guns blocked any attempt to land troops there. Even if troops could land, the bluffs rose too high for the men to climb and capture the city.

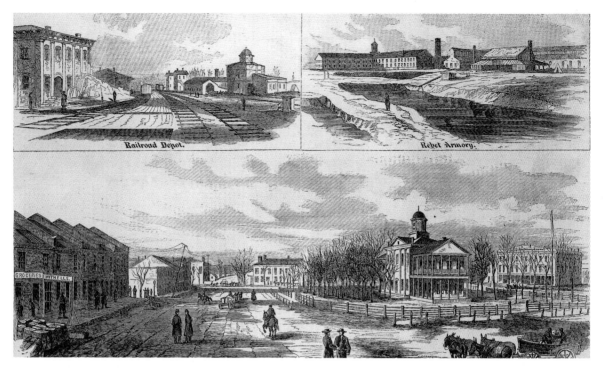

Railroad Depot.

Rebel Armory.

GROCERIES MITHELLS

Views of Holly Springs before the Confederate raid, which destroyed $1.5 million in Union army supplies.

Union forces could approach the city from the west, but the swampy land there would slow any advance on foot. In addition, the army eventually had to cross the river because the city was on the east. The land on the east bank was drier and more even, making it easier to march and fight there, but Vicksburg's defenders had trenches and fortifications to prevent attacks on that side.

Grant's First Attempt at Vicksburg

Ulysses S. Grant first tried to march to Vicksburg down the eastern edge of the river. In late 1862, he brought his army down from western Tennessee.

He established a base at the town of Holly Springs and moved south along a rail line so he could stay supplied. Eventually, however, Grant's army was 150 miles (240 km) from its base, which made it vulnerable to Confederate raids.

Confederate cavalry commander Nathan Bedford Forrest attacked Grant's supply line. Striking quickly and often, Forrest had his troops break up rail lines, tear up telegraph lines, and capture or destroy Union supplies. They also wounded or killed two thousand Union soldiers. Adding insult to injury, another Confederate cavalry force destroyed the supply depot at Holly Springs.

Nathan Bedford Forrest was a self-taught cavalry genius whose strategy in war was simple: "get thar fust [there first] with the most men."

Sherman's failed attack against the strong Confederate defenses at Chickasaw Bluffs cost him nearly eighteen hundred soldiers compared to only two hundred defenders.

Grant was forced to retreat back to Tennessee. On the way, he and his men raided Confederate farms for food and **forage** for their horses. For Grant, this was a good lesson—an army did not need a supply train if it could live off the land.

Union Failure in Battle

While Forrest and the Confederacy were frustrating Grant on the Mississippi's eastern shore, Grant's colleague William Tecumseh Sherman was having his own problems. Major

General Sherman had led another Union force to the Vicksburg area. The plan had been for him to attack at the same time as Grant. Grant was to move against Vicksburg itself, while Sherman was supposed to hit the Confederate defenses on Chickasaw Bluffs north of the city.

Since Grant's telegraph lines had been cut, he could not tell Sherman that he had withdrawn. Sherman, then, went ahead with his attack. On December 29, 1862, he threw 20,000 soldiers against about 14,000 Confederate defenders. The Confederates were in a strong defensive position on high ground, which made the attack difficult. They mowed down the attacking Northerners.

Sherman saw the hopelessness of the situation and called off the attack. A few days later, he pulled back.

Failed Approaches

Early in 1863, Grant moved his head-quarters to Milliken's Bend, upriver from Vicksburg but on the western shore. Sherman and his men were also there, giving Grant about 45,000 troops.

Grant decided to try engineering for his next approach. The Mississippi River made a deep loop opposite Vicksburg; Grant's men started digging a canal that would cut through this loop. This way, he could move his army by water from north of Vicksburg to the south, land on the river's eastern shore, and march against the city's defenses from there.

Grant's soldiers labored on the canal for weeks, but high water from winter rains made the task too difficult. In March of 1863, he abandoned the project. A similar effort aimed at creating a canal farther north also failed as it became clear that the digging would take too long.

Two other attempts tried to use the Union navy. In both, Grant sent boats up rivers that fed into the Mississippi on the eastern side. He hoped the boats could land troops that could approach Vicksburg from the side. Neither of those attempts worked. The rivers were too narrow and the nearby trees and other vegetation too tangled to let the boats pass. The Confederates also moved forces into the area to block the boats.

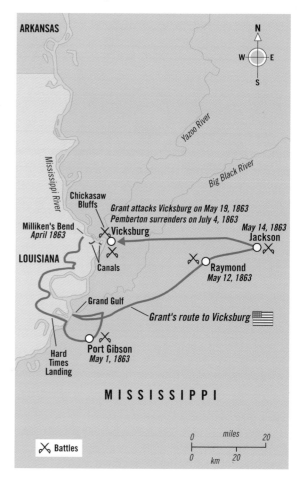

Sherman's December 1862 attack on Chicka-saw Bluffs, just north of Vicksburg, failed, preventing the Union from gaining a foothold near the city. Grant was forced to spend several months trying different ways of getting at Vicksburg. He succeeded only when he crossed the river far south of the city.

A New Plan

Finally, Grant hit on a workable plan. Gathering his army at Milliken's Bend, he marched it along the western shores of the river to a point well south of Vicksburg. Meanwhile, a naval fleet scurried past the fortress. Then it could ferry the Union soldiers across the river to the eastern shore.

Once his troops were on the eastern shore on April 30, 1863, Grant moved quickly. The next day, he captured Port Gibson. Then, he struck east. Joseph Johnston, he knew, was gathering an army at Jackson, Mississippi, east of Vicksburg. Before that force could be used against him, Grant smashed through the Confederate troops. Then he quickly moved on Vicksburg, winning two small battles to bring his army to the outskirts of the city.

In June 1863, Confederate forces attacked Grant's supply base at Milliken's Bend in a small but fierce battle. Union soldiers repelled the assault.

The Confederates at Vicksburg, commanded by John Pemberton, were reeling. As they retreated back into the

Union soldiers pour over part of Vicksburg's defenses in a battle in May 1863. In the end, Grant's army had to surround the city and try to starve its defenders into surrendering.

city, one Southern woman described them as "wan, hollow-eyed, ragged, [and] footsore." Grant gave them no rest; he struck with his whole army on May 19. The Confederates had strong defenses, though, and could not be ousted. A May 22 attack brought the same result—heavy Union casualties and no break in Vicksburg's defenses. The Southern defenders of Vicksburg were still formidable.

City Under Siege

Unable to overrun the Confederate defenders, Grant had no choice but to put the city under **siege**. With his armies surrounding it, he made sure that no supplies could get in. Days dragged into weeks, and weeks stretched on. Still Vicksburg's defenders and about three thousand civilians held out. Soldiers were issued only one-quarter of a day's **rations** as the army tried to make its little food last as long as possible. People began to eat whatever they could, including dogs, cats, mules, and rats.

Surrender

The Southerners in Vicksburg hoped that Joe Johnston would bring **reinforcements** and rescue them. Johnston did not think he had enough troops, however, and felt that Vicksburg would have to be given up.

A MEDAL OF HONOR

During the May 22 attack, Union soldier Thomas H. Higgins showed such bravery that he won a Medal of Honor. His Confederate foes both saved his life and made that medal possible.

When Higgins's regiment attacked the Confederate defenses at Vicksburg, withering Southern fire cut down all of the attackers. Only Higgins, carrying the Union flag, remained standing. Though all alone, he kept on coming. The Confederates were moved by his courage and stopped shooting. Higgins advanced all the way to the Southern lines, where he was taken prisoner amid Southern cheers. After the war, the Confederate soldiers recommended that Congress give Higgins the medal.

The desperate situation inside Vicksburg became clear on June 28. Pemberton was given a message authored by "Many Soldiers" that said, "If you can't feed us, you had better surrender, horrible as the idea is, [rather] than suffer this noble army to disgrace themselves by desertion. . . . This army is now ripe for mutiny, unless it can be fed." On July 3, 1863, Pemberton surrendered his force.

"No word of exultation was uttered to irritate the feelings of the prisoners. On the contrary, every [soldier] who came upon posts brought a [knapsack] filled with provisions, which he would give to some famished Southerner with the remark, 'Here, Reb, I know you are starved nearly to death.'"

Sergeant William Tunnard,
Confederate army at
Vicksburg

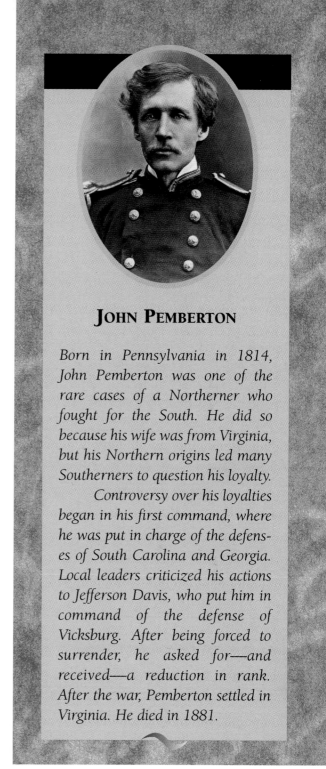

John Pemberton

Born in Pennsylvania in 1814, John Pemberton was one of the rare cases of a Northerner who fought for the South. He did so because his wife was from Virginia, but his Northern origins led many Southerners to question his loyalty.

Controversy over his loyalties began in his first command, where he was put in charge of the defenses of South Carolina and Georgia. Local leaders criticized his actions to Jefferson Davis, who put him in command of the defense of Vicksburg. After being forced to surrender, he asked for—and received—a reduction in rank. After the war, Pemberton settled in Virginia. He died in 1881.

The Impact

The loss of Vicksburg doomed Port Hudson downriver. It had been besieged for weeks; its defenders were as miserable as those at Vicksburg. Six days after Pemberton, they surrendered, too. The Mississippi River was now completely open to Union shipping.

Bitter over the loss of Vicksburg, Davis blamed both Pemberton's army and Joe Johnston, a general, he said, "who wouldn't fight." In the North, meanwhile, the Fourth of July, 1863, was a happy day. Northerners celebrated both the fall of Vicksburg and the defeat of Lee at Gettysburg as well. The tide of war seemed to have turned in favor of the Union.

1860 *Nov. 6:* Lincoln wins presidential election by sweeping North.
Dec. 20: South Carolina secedes.

1861 *Apr. 12:* Fort Sumter is shelled; surrenders on April 13; marks beginning of Civil War.
Aug. 10: Confederate victory at Wilson's Creek in Missouri.

1862 *Feb. 6:* Union victory at Fort Henry, Tennessee.
Feb. 16: Union victory at Fort Donelson, Tennessee.
Feb. 21: Confederate victory at Valverde, New Mexico Territory.
Mar. 14: Surrender of Confederate fort at New Madrid, Missouri.
Mar. 26: Victory at Glorieta Pass gives Union control of New Mexico.
Apr. 6–7: Union victory at Shiloh, Tennessee; Albert Sidney Johnston killed in battle.
Apr. 8: Capture of Island No. 10 gives Union control of northern Mississippi River.
Apr. 24: Farragut's fleet passes forts St. Philip and Jackson, ensuring Union capture of New Orleans.
May 7–8: Victory at Pea Ridge, Arkansas, gives Union control of lands west of Mississippi River.
May 29: General P. G. T. Beauregard has his Confederate troops abandon Corinth, Mississippi.
June 6: Union navy captures Memphis, Tennessee.
Aug. 30: Confederate victory at Richmond threatens Kentucky.
Sep. 2: Confederates capture Lexington, Kentucky.

Sep. 17: Confederate victory at Mumfordville, Kentucky.
Oct. 4: Union captures Galveston, Texas.
Oct. 8: Union victory at Perrysville, Kentucky, ends Confederate invasion.
Oct. 24: Lincoln replaces Union general Don Carlos Buell with Major General William Rosecrans.
Oct. 24: Grant abandons first advance on Vicksburg and retreats.
Dec. 20: Grant abandons second advance on Vicksburg and retreats.
Dec. 29: Confederate victory at Chickasaw Bluffs, Mississippi, halts Union advance on Vicksburg.
Dec. 31: First day of fighting at Stones River, Tennessee.

1863 *Jan. 1:* Confederates recapture Galveston, Texas.
Jan. 2: Second day of fighting at Stones River.
May 1: Union captures Port Gibson, Mississippi.
May 14: Union victory at Jackson, Mississippi, opens final Vicksburg campaign.
May 16: Union victory at Champion Hill, Mississippi.
July 3: Confederates at Vicksburg, Mississippi, surrender.
July 4: Northerners celebrate fall of Vicksburg and defeat of Lee at Gettysburg.
July 9: Confederates at Port Hudson, Louisiana, surrender, giving Union control of the Mississippi River.
Sep. 8: Confederate victory at Sabine Pass blocks Union advance on Texas.

artillery: large, heavy weapons such as cannons; also used to refer to the branch of the army that uses such weapons.

blockade: to prevent enemy ships from carrying goods into or out of ports during a war by blocking a port with ships.

Border States: the states on the northern edge of the southern states, where there was slavery, but it was not a very strong part of society; includes Delaware, Maryland, Kentucky, and Missouri.

campaign: a series of army movements aimed at achieving a particular objective.

casualties: people killed, wounded, captured, and missing in a battle.

Confederacy: also called "the South;" another name for the Confederate States of America, the nation formed by the states that had seceded—Virginia, Tennessee, North Carolina, South Carolina, Georgia, Alabama, Mississippi, Louisiana, Texas, Arkansas, and Florida.

division: an army unit that included troops from about ten to fifteen regiments and totaled about ten thousand soldiers.

forage: food for animals.

Freedmen's Bureau: a government organization established in 1865 to oversee assistance and protection for former slaves.

guerrillas: fighters who are not part of a regular army and who strike quickly by surprise and then escape.

militia: a military unit containing citizens who volunteer for duty temporarily.

Old Northwest: the states that emerged from the Northwest Territory, which were formed in the 1780s, including Ohio, Indiana, Illinois, Michigan, Wisconsin, and Minnesota.

ration: a fixed portion of food given to a soldier over a set period of time.

regiment: a unit of soldiers that included ten companies that were commanded by a colonel; in battle, regiments rarely reached their desired strength of one thousand due to losses from earlier battles.

reinforcements: soldiers added to a force to make it stronger.

secede: to leave the Union.

siege: surrounding and bombarding a fortified position with artillery; this prevents food or supplies from reaching the enemy so they are forced to surrender.

Union: also called "the North;" another name for the United States of America, which, after secession, included Maine, New Hampshire, Vermont, Massachusetts, Rhode Island, Connecticut, New York, New Jersey, Pennsylvania, Delaware,

Maryland, Ohio, Michigan, Indiana, Illinois, Kentucky, Wisconsin, Minnesota, Iowa, Kansas, Missouri, Oregon, and California; in 1863, West Virginia seceded from Virginia and entered the Union as a separate state.

Unionist: a person in the South who supported the Union.

West Point: the United States Military Academy, located in West Point, New York, where cadets are trained in military arts.

Further Resources

These web sites and books cover the fighting in the west from 1861 to 1863 and the people who played roles in that part of the war:

WEB SITES

www.civil-war.net The Civil War Home Page web site includes selected documents by Lincoln and others, including entries of soldiers' diaries and letters home, a detailed time line, and images of war.

www.civilwaralbum.com The Civil War Album includes modern and wartime photos of Civil War sites and maps.

www.homepages.dsu.edu/jankej/civilwar/ civilwar.htm An index web site lists numerous articles on a wide range of Civil War topics. Also includes way to search for individual Civil War soldiers and sailors.

www.nps.gov/stri Stones River National Battlefield homepage.

www.nps.gov/vick Take an online tour of Vicksburg National Military Park's major sites.

www.pbs.org/wgbh/amex/lincolns A companion web site to the PBS special, *The Time of the Lincolns*. It covers politics, slavery, and a "woman's world."

sunsite.utk.edu/civil-war/warweb.html The American Civil War web site contains a number of links to resources, including images of wartime, Civil War re-enactors, and biographical information.

BOOKS

Arnold, James R., and Roberta Weiner. *On to Richmond: The Civil War in the West*, 1861-1863. (The Civil War). Minneapolis: Lerner, 2002.

Bolotin, Norman. *The Civil War A to Z : A Young Readers' Guide to over 100 People, Places, and Points of Importance*. New York: Dutton, 2002.

Clinton, Catherine. *Scholastic Encyclopedia of the Civil War.* New York: Scholastic Books, 1999.

Editors of Time-Life. *The Time-Life History of the Civil War.* New York: Barnes and Noble Books, 1995.

Frazier, Joey. *Jefferson Davis: Confederate President* (Famous Figures of the Civil War Era). Philadelphia: Chelsea House, 2001.

Kirchberger, Joe. *The Civil War and Reconstruction: An Eyewitness History.* New York: Facts On File, 1991.

Index

Page numbers in *italics* indicate maps and diagrams.